NATIONAL GEOGRAPHIC KiDS

EVERYTHING PETS

Hamster

This Labrador mixed breed makes a good friend.

EVERYTHING
PETS

BY JAMES SPEARS

WITH PET EXPERT VIRGINIA MORELL

NATIONAL GEOGRAPHIC

WASHINGTON, D.C.

CONTENTS

Fuzzy ferrets may look like rodents, but they're actually related to weasels and minks.

This red-eared slider turtle may not seem like it takes a lot of work, but turtles need a lot of care. Turtles can live for decades and can grow to over a foot (30.5 cm) long!

INTRODUCTION

WHETHER YOU LIKE TO

DRIVE YOUR CAT CRAZY WITH A LASER
pointer, make faces at the fish in your aquarium, or toss a slobbery tennis ball to your pup, your pet is your BFF!

People and animals have had a close relationship for at least 30,000 years, and there are millions of pets in the world today. Cats and dogs were probably the first pets, but people have long enjoyed caring for other animals as well. Fish and horses, for example, have lived with people for thousands of years. All of today's pets are distant cousins of animals once used for food, protection, or hard work. But the animals we have as pets today became more than a meal or a furry tractor—they became companions. There is a lot to know about these faithful friends, so Sit! Stay! And get ready to learn EVERYTHING about pets.

EXPLORER'S CORNER

HI, I'M VIRGINIA MORELL.

I'm an author and science correspondent for National Geographic. One of my favorite things is studying what goes on in animals' minds. I meet so many animals with such interesting behaviors. Some are pets and some are not. Our pets, the animals we live with such as dogs, cats, and goldfish, are often like special members of the family. Even if they can't talk to us, we often enjoy telling them our secrets; sometimes, they seem to understand us better than anyone else in the world.

Look for me and my collie, Buck, throughout the book for a behind-the-scenes glance at the world of pets!

Green-winged macaw

Cockatiel

Tortoiseshell kitten

Milk snake

Harlequin Great Dane

Chocolate and white
Chihuahua puppy

Hamster

Ferret

1

PETS ON PARADE

Maine coon cat

Rabbit

Clownfish

Pets are animals that people keep as companions. Around the world people agree: Cats, dogs, birds, fish, and reptiles make great pets.

WHAT ARE PETS?

A modern breed called an Egyptian Mau

DO YOU CONSIDER

THE FAMILY CAT YOUR BEST BUD?

We all know how fiercely loyal cat lovers can be to their pets. But 5,000 years ago in Egypt, people went a step further and even considered cats sacred. The goddess Bastet was represented as a cat. Egyptians buried cat mummies as offerings to the goddess hoping she might do them a favor or two. It's likely Egyptians noticed that cats were also pretty useful to have around the house since cats could drive out rats, snakes, and other pests. Over time, people began to take care of cats as pets. These cats became domesticated, or tamed—though some people would say you can never really tame a cat!

Although some animals were worshipped, most of today's pets come from animals that helped humans in some way. Dogs helped people hunt wild animals and protected the hunters at night. Guinea pigs and rabbits were first raised for food. Horses helped people carry heavy loads and get where they wanted to go.

So what makes an animal a pet? Well, people think of pets as members of the family. We feed them and care for them just because they make us feel good.

A statue of the Egyptian goddess Bastet

160 million

86 million

78 million

16 million

13 million

8 million

Guppy

PETS THAT LEAD THE PACK

How popular are pets in the United States? Millions of people have them. Take a look at how many different animals are owned as pets in the U.S.

Domestic shorthair

Mixed breed

Bearded dragon

Thoroughbred

Budgerigar

Fish

Cats

Dogs

Birds

Reptiles

Horses

WHAT ISN'T A PET?

Livestock aren't.
Livestock are animals that people use only for food or work, or for their hair, hide, or fur. Some examples are goats raised for milk, oxen used to plow fields, or sheep bred for wool. Livestock owners take care of the animals to make sure they are healthy, but most farmers won't let their dairy cow sleep at the foot of the bed.

Wild animals aren't.
Some people try to tame wild animals such as raccoons or wolves, but these animals are not pets. Wild animals often show aggressive behaviors, which make them good at surviving in nature but not so good at playing nice with family members or being polite at the dinner table. It's also hard to meet a wild animal's needs, such as having enough outdoor space to roam. Not meeting an animal's needs can harm its health and make it unhappy.

Wolf

FURRY FACT CRICKETS ARE POPULAR PETS IN CHINA.

COOL CATS AND HOT DOGS

WHEN YOU SPOT A TEACUP

CHIHUAHUA POKING ITS HEAD OUT OF A FANCY purse, it's hard to imagine it's related to wolves. But it's true! The first dogs were likely wolves that began getting used to living around people more than 30,000 years ago. Dogs were the first pets that people had, and it's easy to understand why they became man's (and woman's) best friend. Once dogs teamed up with people, they did everything from protecting the family to herding livestock to even pulling carts. They still do those things and much more!

When it comes to cats, the ancient Egyptians aren't the only people to have loved them. Cats are one of the world's most popular pets, with over 400 million in the world. Just as with dogs, there are many kinds of cats. Some are thin and sleek, like the Russian Blue, while others are thick and fluffy, like the Persian cat. Cats and dogs are found on every continent except Antarctica—a true sign of their world-class appeal.

Rottweiler

Chihuahua

AAARRRR!

If you picture a parrot perched on every pirate's shoulder, think again. Cats have long ruled the high seas as sailors' friends. These living mousetraps kept stowaway rodents from chewing up ropes or wood or getting into food supplies. Safe food meant healthy sailors. Food contaminated by rats meant a ship full of sick people. Cats also made affectionate companions for seafaring travelers who were away from family and friends for months at a time.

American shorthair cat

THE UGLIEST DOG IN THE WORLD

Meet Mugly, the 2012 champ for World's Ugliest Dog. Mugly is a Chinese crested terrier—a breed that often takes first prize in ugly-dog contests everywhere. So what's the appeal of this pup that looks like the star of a horror movie? For one, the lack of hair makes it a good choice for people with allergies. And according to their owners, these dogs are so ugly . . . they're downright cute.

Russian blue cat

FURRY FACT THE WORLD'S SMALLEST DOG LIVES IN KENTUCKY AND IS SMALLER THAN A SODA CAN.

HAPPY AND HAIRY

CATS AND DOGS AREN'T THE

ONLY FUR BALLS WE ADORE. People are crazy about many other mammals, including rabbits, horses, and rodents.

A RABBIT HABIT

Rabbits have been prized for their meat and fur for almost a thousand years, but around the 1800s, people began keeping rabbits as pets. There are close to 50 different breeds of rabbits. Besides being cuddly, rabbits are easy to care for. Some can learn to fetch like a dog and to use a litter box like a cat.

RODENT ROUNDUP

Some kids might squeak with joy or eek in fear at the sight of a mouse or rat. But from classrooms to bedrooms, these small mammals remain popular pets.

Angora rabbit

GUINEA PIG

Originally raised for food in South America, guinea pigs were brought to Europe by Spanish explorers in the 1500s. There they became house pets.

GERBIL

These desert rodents originally came from Africa and Asia. They have only been pets for about 50 years or so. Gerbils are extremely active at night.

FURRY FACT   THE WORLD'S LARGEST PET RABBIT IS A CONTINENTAL GIANT NAMED DARIUS. HE WEIGHS 50 POUNDS (23 KG).

HORSE PLAY

Horses were first hunted for meat. Then some 5,000 years ago people began to tame them and harness them for riding and pulling carts and plows. But horses were made to run. Some run faster than 30 miles an hour (48 kph) and jump as high as 7 feet (2 m)! People discovered how fun it was to ride along, so horses starting becoming pets to ride around on. Added bonus: They're the only all-terrain vehicles that run on oats instead of gasoline.

EXPLORER'S CORNER

Do you have a rat as a pet? Guess what? Rats laugh. Here's what scientists have found out: Rats open their mouths when they play together. No one could hear a sound when they did this, so everyone assumed it was just the way rats play. Then one scientist put a special device near the cage where the rats were playing. The device transformed the rats' sounds for our human ears. What do you suppose the scientist heard? Laughter! The rats laughed in very high, happy squeaks. Just like us, rats laugh when they play together.

CHINCHILLA

These balls of pure softness are actually related to prickly porcupines—go figure. To "bathe" themselves, chinchillas roll around in dust, which dries their fur and keeps it soft and beautiful. Nothing like a good dust bath!

HAMSTER

Hamsters have terrible eyesight but their senses of smell and touch, as well as their whiskers, help them navigate.

MOUSE AND RAT

Humans often consider wild mice and rats to be terrible pests. But as pets, these rodents rock! Rats are generally two to three times as big as mice and live a year or two longer. Like all rodents, mice and rats are gnawers—they must chew constantly to keep their teeth ground down.

FINS, SCALES, AND FEATHERS

Blue and gold macaw

FURRY FACT THE WORLD'S LARGEST RECORDED GOLDFISH WAS OVER A FOOT (30 CM) LONG AND LIVED IN THE NETHERLANDS.

NOT EVERYONE IS MOVED BY MAMMALS.

For folks who fancy feathers and fins over fur, the best pets may slither, squawk, or swim.

Goldfish

FRIENDLY FISH

Long before there were television screens to stare at, there were fishponds and aquariums! More than 2,000 years ago Romans kept fishponds, and many cultures think having pet fish brings good luck. There are two types of fish: freshwater and saltwater. Freshwater fish, including goldfish and bettas, are easier to care for in an aquarium at home than many saltwater fish are. But salty or not, fish are relaxing to watch.

Siamese fighting, or betta, fish

BIRDS WITH BRAINS

All pet owners talk to their pets, but not every pet talks back! Some birds have the gift of gab, and many species of parrots learn dozens of words and phrases. Some of these master mimics can sound like a car honking or phone ringing.

Lovebirds

RAVISHING REPTILES

Green iguana

People have been charmed by—and charming—snakes for thousands of years. Reptiles such as snakes and lizards are becoming more popular pets than dogs in countries like England. Reptiles don't need the attention or exercise that cats and dogs do, so they're good pets for busy people.

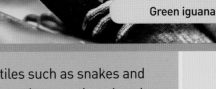

Ball python, aka royal python

PHOTOGRAPHIC DIAGRAMS

CLOSE-UP OF CATS AND DOGS

Whiskers Cats' whiskers are extremely sensitive. They help cats sense where they are in narrow, dark spaces when there isn't enough light to see. The whiskers brush against the wall, letting the cat know if it can fit its body through the space. This makes it possible for cats to hunt rodents and snakes in tight places.

Tail When cats walk along the tops of fences or other skinny surfaces, they use their tails to help them balance. Tail position can also signal, "Let's play!" or "I'm ready to pounce."

American shorthair cat

Skeleton Cats have no collarbone, which gives them a flexible skeleton. This means they can twist and turn, even in midair, like when they flip their bodies during a fall, trying to land on their feet.

Claws Cats' claws are curved, helping them get a grip on prey—and curtains! The claws are also attached to muscles in the cats' paws so they can be retracted when they are not needed.

FROM WHISKERS TO TAILS,
BOTH CATS AND DOGS HAVE TRAITS THAT HELP
them sense the world, hunt, move, and communicate. Check out how they have adapted to their environments!

Coat Many dog breeds have two coats—a rough outer coat and a soft undercoat. These coats help keep them warm and dry, like a built-in sweater and rain jacket.

Tail Some snow dogs, such as Alaskan malamutes, use their tails as scarves that they drape over their faces to stay warm and protected from the snow.

Nose A dog's nose is over a thousand times more sensitive than a person's nose. Scientists say that dogs can smell odors that people can't. Dogs can even smell some illnesses in people, such as certain cancers!

Paws The pads on the bottom of a dog's paws are tough. These tough pads help to protect the dog's feet from injury on rough ground. The fatty tissue on the pads makes them comfortable to walk on, like the fluff of a comfy slipper.

Norwich terrier

Pets need a safe place to play, sleep, and eat. Some homey habitats are simple cages. Others, such as this hamster haven, can be the ultimate pet paradise.

CREATURE
COMFORTS

PAMPERED PETS

MANICURES!

MASSAGES!

CLOTHING!

GYM MEMBERSHIPS!

MANIS AND PEDIS—AND A WHOLE LOT MORE—SOME PETS REALLY ENJOY LIFE! Gunther IV is a German shepherd worth more than $300 million, thanks to a countess who left her entire fortune to her pets. Gunther is not the only millionaire mutt, either. Trouble the Maltese became famous after receiving $12 million from his owner. He lived in a New York penthouse and was driven in a limousine to get a pedicure once a week.

With $12 million in the bank, Trouble is one pampered pooch.

Other pets have cashed in, too. A pet chicken named Gigoo inherited $10 million and a countryside estate from her owner in England.

People have adorned their pets with gold and jewelry for thousands of years, and for the very wealthy and their animal companions, the sky is the limit. From designer water bowls to pet beds woven with real gold fibers, money can buy just about anything for our animal friends. In fact, today's super-rich pet owners have more options than ever for spoiling their pets.

FURRY FACT TINKERBELL THE CHIHUAHUA HAS A DOGGY MANSION WITH A CHANDELIER, SPIRAL STAIRCASE, AND AIR-CONDITIONING.

FURNITURE!

DESIGNER DUDS

If you think people are the only ones who wear expensive threads, think again. Whether it's a mink coat for a cat or a $1,000 designer tracksuit for Fido's morning walk, pet clothes are big business. Some even wear diamond-studded collars that cost over a million dollars!

JEWELRY!

Annual Pet Spending
(all figures are U.S. in 2011)

$19.9 BILLION
Food

$13.4 BILLION
Veterinary care

$11.8 BILLION
Supplies and nonprescription medicine

$3.8 BILLION
Pet services: grooming and boarding

$2.1 BILLION
Purchase of animals

SPAS FOR SPANIELS

Chasing balls at the park all day can be exhausting, which is why there are hotels and spas dedicated exclusively to pets. The Pooch Hotel in Los Angeles is one of the fanciest dog spas in the world. For $125 a night, a dog gets a suite with a flat-panel television for entertainment and a webcam so the owner can watch the doggy from a distance. Guest pets even get a free massage or special playtime at the pool.

PIG AND PUP PALS

That cute creature on the right is a wild boar piglet and his pal is a Jack Russell terrier named Candy. The piglet was starving in a field in Germany: He was only a few weeks old, and his mother was nowhere to be found. Candy's family found the piglet, named him Manni, and bottle-fed him to keep him alive. Once Manni was out of danger, he and Candy started to play with each other every day. They liked hide-and-seek and just general romping around. And the two learned to communicate too. Manni took up barking like Candy. Of course, a wild boar is a wild boar, so Manni couldn't stay with Candy forever. But it was fun while it lasted!

ANIMAL BUDDIES

KOKO AND HER KITTEN

Koko, a lowland gorilla that lives in California, is famous for knowing more than a thousand words in sign language. She also loves kittens! Her first pet cat was a Manx that she named All Ball. Manx cats have no tails, which is probably why Koko thought it looked like a ball. She raised several kittens, and loved to play with them. Some grew up and moved away, and then Koko would adopt another kitten.

WHAT DO YOU GET WHEN **AN ORANGUTAN CROSSES PATHS WITH A HOUND DOG?** Best friends! Suryia, an orangutan, and Roscoe, a bluetick hound, met in South Carolina at a preserve for endangered animals. Roscoe was hungry and homeless and wandered into the park looking for food. Suryia found Roscoe and immediately adopted the dog. The two have been best buddies ever since. Suryia even takes Roscoe for a walk every day.

Animals can and often do get along if they are raised together or if they have compatible personalities. Like people, many animals love having friends.

FURRY FACT KOKO ALSO MADE FRIENDS WITH A PARROT. SHE NAMED IT DEVIL TOOTH BECAUSE IT WAS RED AND HAD A BEAK.

PLAYTHINGS
FOR PETS

WHY DO KITTENS BAT AT PIECES OF STRING?
WHY CAN SOME DOGS CHASE A BALL A BILLION TIMES AND NOT GET TIRED?

Why do hamsters run on wheels? Just like people, pets love to play! Some playful behavior, like when hamsters run on wheels, is just exercise. Other play behavior shows animals using their smarts: Cats playing with toys or dogs wrestling at the park is behavior that comes from an animal's wilder side. This type of play is practice for hunting for food—something wild ancestors needed to do to survive. Animals love activity, and being involved in your pet's exercise allows you to bond and have fun!

Crazy About Catnip

Have you ever seen a cat go bonkers around catnip? This mint has a funny effect on felines. A chemical in the plant causes most cats—from tabbies to tigers—to go bananas. Cats will roll in the plant, lick it, eat it, and begin to jump around. And then, after a couple of minutes, the effect wears off, and the cat acts like nothing unusual ever happened.

Play With a Fish?

Mirror, mirror on the wall, who's the bravest fish of all? That would be the Siamese fighting fish, also known as the betta. When you show a male betta its own reflection, the fish will usually puff up and display its brilliant fins in an attempt to scare off this "rival."

THERE'S A (Y)APP FOR THAT

When it comes to toys, today's pets think electronics are purr-fect. In the app "Game for Cats," felines swat images that move across the screen. Good eye-paw coordination nets points, and cats can even compete across the Internet to see who is the best virtual mouser. For dogs, there is the "Dog Toy" app, which squeaks like a real chew toy. But keep an eye on your phone or tablet so it doesn't get eaten!

EXPLORER'S CORNER

My dog, Buck, and I live in wide, open country in Oregon. We take hikes in the forest near our home. Buck likes to lead the way; it's his way of protecting me. In the winter, we go cross-country skiing together in the mountains and hills. Buck wears special boots to protect his feet from the snow and ice, just like I do. Buck never gets tired of learning new tricks: Some of his favorites are chasing big sticks and playing dead. We took a class together called "agility training for dogs," and I learned how to guide Buck to jump over fences and through a tire, and to run through a tunnel.

Blue budgerigar, or budgie parakeet

Up for a Game of Bird Ball?

Parrots and parakeets don't spend all day gabbing. In order to keep up their feathered physique, these birds love to play with toys. Smart and sporty, parrots can learn to play with a ball, even putting it through a hoop. Maybe one day you'll see a parrot in the NBA.

English springer spaniel

A hamster peeks out of its roller ball, a toy that helps it get exercise!

FURRY FACT   A HAMSTER'S FILLED CHEEK POUCHES EXTEND PAST ITS SHOULDERS.

PETS THAT PROTECT

ANIMALS AREN'T JUST

GOOD COMPANIONS—SOMETIMES THEY CAN BE REAL LIFESAVERS. Throughout history there have been stories of pets showing courage and sacrifice to stay with or comfort people who needed help. Dogs and horses have often played important roles during times of war and disaster. Horses have been used in the military for thousands of years, and a dog's nose is one of the best tools for finding people who are trapped in the rubble of destroyed buildings in natural disasters.

WAR HORSE

Between 356 and 323 B.C., an enormous black stallion named Bucephalus helped Alexander the Great create one of the greatest empires in history. When Bucephalus died, Alexander buried the horse and named a city in its honor. Since then, horses have continued to play an important part in warfare. In 2011, horses used in the War in Afghanistan were honored with a statue near the site of the former World Trade Center in New York City— the target of the attack that started the war.

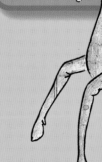

FROM HOMELESS TO HERO

Pearl is a black Labrador retriever who had a rough start. Her first family couldn't keep her, so they gave her to an animal shelter. A worker from a search-dog foundation saw Pearl's potential and adopted her. Pearl became a search-and-rescue dog, and she spent over two weeks in Haiti after the devastating 2010 earthquake there. Pearl found 12 people trapped in rubble, saving all of their lives! Pearl went to Japan to help search for people trapped after the 2011 earthquake and tsunami.

Search-and-rescue teams all over the world use specially trained dogs to search for survivors. This smart-sniffing golden retriever helps after a deadly earthquake in Van, Turkey, in 2011.

FURRY FACT SPECIAL FLUID ON THE TIP OF A DOG'S NOSE HELPS TO CATCH SCENT MOLECULES.

A PHOTO GALLERY

SAY FLEAS!

PETS ARE SOCIAL

AND ENJOY GOOD COMPANY.

Whether they're cuddling with their own mothers, hanging out with you, or talking among themselves, pets are happier and healthier when they have good friends, good food, and lots to do.

Mother cats nurse their kittens until they're ready to eat other food.

Conures are known as clowns of the parrot world. They often bob their heads and sway back and forth.

Ancient relatives of the Chihuahua were sacred pets of the Maya, Toltec, and Aztec cultures.

A chameleon's tongue can extend up to two times the length of its body.

Chinchillas have about 60 hairs per hair follicle, making their fur very soft. Humans have only one or two.

Most collies have natural herding instincts and can be great ranch or farm companions.

Ball pythons are excellent swimmers. They will inflate their lungs with air in order to float!

Some frogs have a wet or sticky substance on their feet to help them climb trees and cling to surfaces.

Both cats and dogs tend to circle an area two to three times before lying down.

Despite their name, hermit crabs are social creatures that prefer to be with friends.

Gerbils sometimes thump their back feet on the ground. If there is more than one hamster, they will all join in!

Hanging out with your animal buddy — taking a walk, throwing a ball, or even enjoying a sleepy cuddle—helps strengthen your bond and relationship with your pet.

FRIENDS
FOR
LIFE

American shorthair cat

Aila, a capuchin monkey, retrieves a disc from a CD player for Travis Roy, who became a quadraplegic in 1995 after an accident during his young hockey career.

GREAT THERAPY: A HORSE AND A SADDLE

It's called hippotherapy, or therapeutic riding. This girl in Huntington Beach, California, gets motor and sensory input from the movements of a horse. That provides her with a combination of physical, occupational, and speech therapy, which helps her a lot in handling some serious challenges: a liver tumor and autism.

A HELPING PAW

HELPER ANIMALS HAVE BEEN AROUND FOR MANY YEARS. DOGS MAKE THE MOST POPULAR assistants, helping people who have problems with sight or hearing. Seeing Eye dogs are among the most common type of service animals. These dogs learn to guide humans across streets, obey traffic lights, and navigate safely wherever they need to go. The dogs spend years learning how to become someone's "eyes." Capuchin monkeys are small and gentle, making them good choices for living in a house with people. They are also intelligent, curious, and natural tool users, which makes them easy to train. Monkeys are trained to help people, especially those who are confined to wheelchairs. Monkeys can flip light switches, retrieve the telephone, and even turn pages in a book—all things that are impossible for a person who might have a paralyzing disease.

A golden retriever guide dog keeps a blind boy active and safe.

Dalmatians are legendary for their roles helping firefighters.

FURRY FACT DALMATIANS WERE FIRST USED BY FIREFIGHTERS IN THE 1700s TO KEEP THIEVES AWAY FROM THEIR WAGONS AND HORSES.

PET SPEAK

A hand signal tells an English bulldog to stay.

LEADER OF THE PACK

If anyone can teach an old dog a new trick, it's Cesar Millan. Cesar began working with aggressive dogs in 1998, and his ability to turn devil dogs into angels earned him worldwide renown. For years, Cesar and his buddy Daddy, a pit bull, traveled across the country helping owners with their problem pooches. Cesar and Daddy even had their own television show that aired in more than 80 countries around the world.

TALKING TO PETS IS NOTHING NEW.

FROM COOING TO A CUDDLY KITTEN IN BABY TALK to disciplining a destructive puppy, we converse with our pets all the time. But do they understand us? Scientists don't think our pets understand language in the same way humans do. Still, many pets are good at reading body language and understanding our moods.

Some pet birds can mimic human speech, though we don't know how much they understand. Others animals, such as dogs, have lived with humans for so long that they seem to understand what we are thinking or feeling. Teaching your dog some tricks, getting your cat to play with a string, or allowing your bird some "shoulder time" are good ways to get in sync with your pet.

FURRY FACT IN 2012, 32 JAPANESE MEDAKA FISH TRAVELED TO THE INTERNATIONAL SPACE STATION.

Treats Do the Trick

Offering rewards is a great way to teach your pet to follow your commands. Just remember to be consistent, and soon your pet will be ready to show off.

An Australian shepherd stands up for a treat.

THE TELLTALE TAIL

Want to know what your cat is thinking? Look at its hind end. The tail is one way a cat lets you know whether it's time to get the treats or to stay back.

Upright tail, not bristled
"Hi there, I'm a cat!"

Tail at rest with tip curved upward
"Life is great!"

Tail curved with a moving tip
"I'm slightly annoyed."

Tail whipping back and forth
"Back off, buddy!"

Upright tail, fully bristled
"Feel my furry wrath! ATTACK!"

WHICH PET TO CHOOSE?

ARE YOU SMITTEN WITH KITTENS OR TANTALIZED BY TARANTULAS?

Deciding on a pet is more than just picking your favorite animal—you have to make sure you are right for each other. Take a look at some of these pets and think about which might be right for you.

WHAT'S UP, DOC?

Animals need checkups, just like people do. It's important to find a good veterinarian in your area who can take care of your pet. Most vets know the basic care of cats and dogs, but if you have finches, frogs, or a pet tarantula, you may need to find a vet who specializes in your type of pet.

Corn Snake

LEVEL OF DIFFICULTY: beginner

HOME SWEET HOME: large glass habitat with a wire top that latches

WHAT IT EATS: mice and rats that are dead

QUICK TIP: To prevent your snake from biting you, feed it with kitchen tongs, and wear a rubber glove. The glove keeps the snake from associating your scent with its dinner.

Guinea Pig

LEVEL OF DIFFICULTY: beginner, with supervision

HOME SWEET HOME: cage with access to food, a toy ball, and soft bedding

WHAT IT EATS: guinea pig pellets, fresh fruits, vegetables, and hay

QUICK TIP: Guinea pigs will whistle and squeak when they are happy. Some will squeal delightedly when they see their owners because that means food is coming.

Parakeet

LEVEL OF DIFFICULTY: beginner

HOME SWEET HOME: a large cage with toys, food, and water

WHAT IT EATS: pellet food and small pieces of fresh fruits and vegetables daily

QUICK TIP: Parakeets can live up to about ten years, so this pet may be the one for you if you want a longtime friend. Parakeets need a lot of interaction and are very social. They are also able to mimic words and noises.

Dog

LEVEL OF DIFFICULTY: intermediate

HOME SWEET HOME: a comfortable spot for sleeping and lots of room for playing

WHAT IT EATS: dog food made mostly from protein, with some grains and vegetables

QUICK TIP: No matter what size dog you choose, be prepared to run and have fun! A dog needs lots of activity every day. Training a dog is also a big part of having one as a pet. Tell your pet "Good dog!" as often as possible, and enjoy the dog kisses that come with the job.

Leopard Wrasse

LEVEL OF DIFFICULTY: expert

HOME SWEET HOME: a 50-gallon saltwater aquarium

WHAT IT EATS: frozen shrimp and other organisms growing in the aquarium.

QUICK TIP: This is a fish that is easily stressed, has a special diet, and is prone to illness in captivity. For aquarists (people who have aquariums), caring for fish with special needs offers a greater challenge.

FURRY FACT RUSSIANS OWN MORE THAN A MILLION PET BIRDS.

"Choose me!" Kittens wait for owners at animal shelters.

PICKING UP YOUR PET

Most animal shelters and pet stores have a wide variety of animals to choose from. When you choose a pet at a shelter, you are rescuing an animal. The downside is that you can't always find a particular breed of cat or dog, and most shelters don't have many fish, birds, or reptiles. Pet stores are excellent places to buy birds, rodents, and fish. Breeders are good choices for people looking for a particular breed of animal, but some breeders worry more about profit than about their animals' health or safety— so it's important to do some research on the breeder first!

Guinea pig

THIS IS NOT A PET

PASS ON THESE PETS

Some animals are never a good idea to keep as pets.

WOLVES: Some people think that wolves are just like dogs and can be kept as pets. Wolves are awesome animals, but they make terrible pets. They are not tame. They're unpredictable around people and may attack them. They also need a lot of space to roam in and can't eat regular pet food.

CHIMPANZEES: Chimps look cute, but when chimps reach adolescence they become much stronger than humans, which makes them difficult to control and possibly dangerous.

POISON DART FROGS: The colorful croakers are beautiful to look at, but they're best seen in photos and on television. In the wild, these animals create a poison that seeps from their skin. They're not usually poisonous when raised in captivity, but they do not like being handled, and many are endangered.

THE IDEA OF RIDING A LION
TO SCHOOL OR TAKING A WOLF FOR A WALK—

or being the only one on the block with a pet chimp or a 12-foot (3.7-m) python—might sound exciting. However, owning a wild animal can end very badly for the animal and the people around it. In the past two decades, hundreds of incidents of injury and death caused by wild animals kept as pets have been reported. In dozens of cases, people have been killed. And in most cases, the animals involved have been destroyed.

If they're so dangerous, why do people keep wild animals? As babies, tigers, wolves, snakes, and other animals seem manageable and cute. But as the animal gets older it grows bigger and stronger and can do real damage.

Some exotic animals are cared for by people in places called sanctuaries. These safe havens often provide a lot of space for the animals to roam in and are closed to the public so that people don't frighten or stress out the animals. Many sanctuaries take animals, such as big cats or primates, that people give up after realizing they're not good pets. The people who work at sanctuaries are usually trained to care for animals properly. They also know how to prepare some of the animals to return to the wild if that's an option.

Bengal tigers may look cute, but they can weigh up to 500 pounds (227 kg) when full grown. That's one big kitty!

EXPLORER'S CORNER

It's so important for us to take care of our animals. As you know, some animals shouldn't be pets, even though they seem like a lot of fun and great companions. Chimps and humans have a special relationship in the science world, and researchers such as Jane Goodall have learned much about chimps by studying them and living with them in the wild. But... guess what? A chimpanzee would be very unhappy in a person's home. It would not have room to roam, or a forest of trees to climb. It would also miss its chimpanzee family and friends. This is true for all wild animals. They need to be in the wild where they can be free.

SNAKES IN THE SWAMP

Burmese pythons are popular snakes for pet owners around the world, but in Florida these snakes are a problem. They might start out as pets, but sometimes they escape into the wild or their owners release them. Once in the wild they can reproduce in large numbers and gobble up the local birds, mammals, and even alligators! In 2005, wildlife researchers in Florida found a Burmese python that had died when it tried to eat a six-foot (1.8-m) alligator.

FURRY FACT A WOMAN NAMED HA WENJIN SOLD EVERYTHING SHE OWNED TO CREATE CHINA'S LARGEST ANIMAL SHELTER.

COMPARING
PETS AND PEOPLE

ALL IN THE FAMILY

HOW MUCH DO
YOU AND YOUR PET HAVE IN
common? Just like us, our pet companions have basic needs, such as food, shelter, proper care, and love! But human relationships with pets often go beyond the ordinary. Dogs have traveled into space, rats are trained to sniff out explosives, and horses help patients feel better. There is no doubt that we humans love all kinds of pets and that these animals are capable of amazing things. We give our pets names, talk to them, and sometimes even dress them in clothes, but how much are pets really like people?

Most health experts think young people should get a minimum of one hour of playtime or exercise every day to stay physically and mentally healthy. Some animals, such as herding dogs, need a lot of exercise to stay happy, while others, such as a box turtle, might be content with a couple laps around the tank.

VS.

Panting Pups
After a game or other form of exercise, you might breathe faster and heavier. Dogs do the same thing. It's called panting, and dogs can pant up to 300 times a minute!

FOOD

Have you ever heard that you shouldn't give people food to a dog or cat? In truth, cats and dogs eat much of the same things people do, including meat, grains, and vegetables. However, cats and dogs eat more protein and less grain than people do.

SENSES

Animals have the same senses as people, but their senses operate differently from ours. Snakes, for example, have an incredible sense of smell in their tongues.

CHILDHOOD

Kids live with their parents for about 18 years before striking out on their own. For pets, that time is much shorter, although the timing depends on when the animal matures.

LIFE SPAN

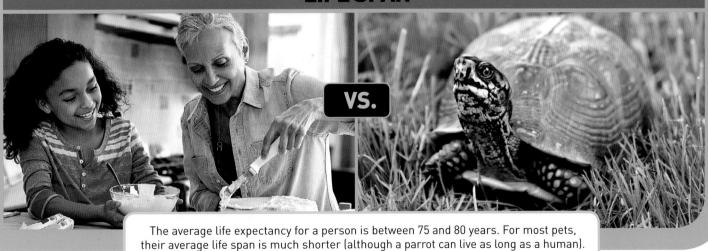

The average life expectancy for a person is between 75 and 80 years. For most pets, their average life span is much shorter (although a parrot can live as long as a human). Fish and reptiles can live for a few years. Dogs and cats often make it to their teens.

4

PET TRICKS

Show-jumping rabbits start training to run and jump through obstacle courses as early as eight weeks old.

BEST IN SHOW

THE MOST FAMOUS DOG SHOW IN THE WORLD is the Westminster Kennel Club Dog Show in New York City. Thousands of dogs from around the world compete to see which one is the finest example of its breed. Since it doesn't make sense to compare poodles to Great Danes, dogs are divided into different classes for competition.

① Sporting
These dogs have a talent for finding or fetching animals during a hunt. For example, a pointer stands still and points its nose toward a bird that is hiding in the brush. Spaniels chase animals out from their hiding spots. Retrievers, as you might guess, retrieve animals that have been shot by hunters.

② Hound
From beagles to bloodhounds, these dogs track people and animals by sight, sound, or scent. Originally considered sporting dogs, hounds got their own class in 1930.

③ Working
These dogs do jobs, from pulling loads to working with the military or the police. Malamutes and Great Danes are two examples of this class.

④ Herding
Shetland sheepdogs and German shepherds fall into this class, along with other dogs that work keeping sheep and cows together in a herd.

⑤ Terrier
Most of these dogs were bred in the United Kingdom, where they tracked down rats and other vermin.

THEY'VE GOT CLASS!

Match the breed of dog on the left to its class on the right. Use the dogs' descriptions as hints.

Dog Breed

A **COLLIE** This dog feels perfectly at home with the animals on a ranch.

B **AKITA** This snow dog pulls heavy loads on sleds.

C **LABRADOR RETRIEVER** With webbed toes and a love for fetching, these dogs are a favorite of duck hunters.

D **JACK RUSSELL** If you think you smell a rat, call on this little pal to get rid of it.

E **TOY POODLE** This mini version of its breed is a total lapdog.

Class

1 Sporting

5 Terrier

6 Toy

4 Herding

3 Working

Answers: A4, B3, C1, D5, E6

6 **Toy**
These dogs were bred for pleasure. Many, from the toy poodle to the Pomeranian, are miniature versions of other breeds.

7 **Non-Sporting**
From bulldogs to poodles, these dogs are no longer used for their original purpose. They have been bred to have many traits but no one skill in particular.

1. Snorkel on boy's head is longer. 2. Rock in the yard is missing. 3. Dog has sunglasses. 4. Girl on left has a hat. 5. Sleeves of girl on right changed color. 6. Dolphin's eye changed color. 7. Garage door windows are missing. 8. Boy's shorts changed color. 9. Cooler is missing. 10. Dog's ring changed color.

SPOT THE DIFFERENCE

Can you spot what's different in these two vacation photos? There are at least ten differences. (Answers are below left.)

FURRY FACT THE WESTMINSTER DOG SHOW, STARTED IN 1877, IS OLDER THAN THE LIGHTBULB.

THE NAME GAME

THE BRIGHT RED FEATHERS OF THE SCARLET MACAW probably give you a good idea where its name comes from. But what about a Rottweiler? Those dogs are named for the German city, Rottweil, where the dog supposedly came from. The dogs originally pulled butcher carts through town. Breed and species names come from a variety of sources. The most common are the animal's appearance or place of origin, the sound it makes, or the job the animal does.

Rottweiler

Scarlet macaw parrot

PET SOUNDS

If someone asked you to moo like a cow, it's no problem. But can you *miau* like a cat? Animals around the world make the same sounds, but people use different words to describe those sounds. Read the sound from each language and guess which animal makes the sound.

1. **piep piep** (Dutch), **eek** (English), **squit** (Italian)

2. **vov vov** (Danish), **wau wau** (German), **vuff vuff** (Finnish)

3. **miaou** (Greek), **miyau** (Russian), **miau** (Spanish)

4. **croa croa** (French), **cra cra** (Italian), **kero kero** (Japanese)

5. **klip klap** (Danish), **paka paka** (Japanese), **cotocloc** (Spanish)

Answers: 1. Mouse, 2. Dog, 3. Cat, 4. Frog, 5. Galloping horse

LIGHTS, CAMERA, ACTION!

Some pets were made for Hollywood. Put on your director's hat, and see if you can match these pets with the movies they appeared in.

1 *Stuart Little*

2 *101 Dalmatians*

3 *Snow Dogs*

4 *Garfield*

A In this 2002 film, a dentist moves to Alaska to compete in a dogsled race.

B A family adopts a well-dressed, talking mouse in this 1999 movie.

C Evil Cruella de Vil wants a coat made from the fur of these dogs.

D The four-legged star of this 2004 movie loves lasagna, hates Mondays, and wishes Odie the dog would move out.

Answers: 1B, 2C, 3A, 4D

PET ROCK

The pet rock became popular in 1975 as a joke gift for people. The rock came in a crate with a manual for helping you train your "new pet." The instructions advised the owner to stick with easy tricks, such as "stay" and "play dead." But the pet rock wasn't the only "non-pet" pet that has been around. See if you can match each "pet" below with its description.

1 Petville
2 Webkinz
3 Tamagotchi
4 Pokémon

A This pet is found on a keychain and hatches from an egg. You press buttons to feed and play with it.

B Short for "pocket monster," these creatures live and train in a top-selling Nintendo game.

C This popular game allows Facebook users to raise pets while updating their status.

D These stuffed animals come and go on the Web. You register your pet and "play" in a virtual world.

Answers: 1C, 2D, 3A, 4B

FURRY FACT A BORDER COLLIE NAMED CHASER UNDERSTANDS MORE THAN A THOUSAND WORDS.

TALL TALES

Bengal cat

CAN YOU GUESS WHICH
OF THESE COMMON BELIEFS ARE FACT AND WHICH ARE MYTH?

A Cats always land on their feet.

B Rabbits can shriek.

C A wet dog nose means the dog is healthy.

D Many kinds of pet birds can learn to talk.

E Dogs are color-blind.

A **MYTH.** While it's true that cats can turn their bodies as they fall, they don't always land on their feet. A cat that doesn't have enough time to twist around before landing can go from "cat" to "splat."

B **FACT.** You might think of bunnies as cute and quiet, but these adorable animals make a horrible noise when they are startled or agitated. This is why it's best not to throw your bunny a surprise party.

Mini Lop rabbit

C **MYTH.** While active, happy dogs often have wet noses, that doesn't tell you much about a dog's health. A dog's nose is often wet because the dog is licking it and because dogs sweat through their noses. But a dog can have a dry nose and be healthy.

Boston terrier

E **MYTH.** Dogs don't see colors as well as people, but scientists are pretty sure dogs can see some colors. They think this because dogs' eyes have some of the same color-detecting cells that people's eyes have.

D **FACT.** Parrots are the most well known for their babbling, but other pet birds, such as the myna, can also mimic human speech. The myna is said to be the best mimic of human speech, but parrots still have the edge for knowing more words.

Cockatiel

Dachshund

FURRY FACT THE OLDEST PET GOLDFISH ON RECORD LIVED FOR 43 YEARS—SO LONG ITS SCALES TURNED SILVER GRAY.

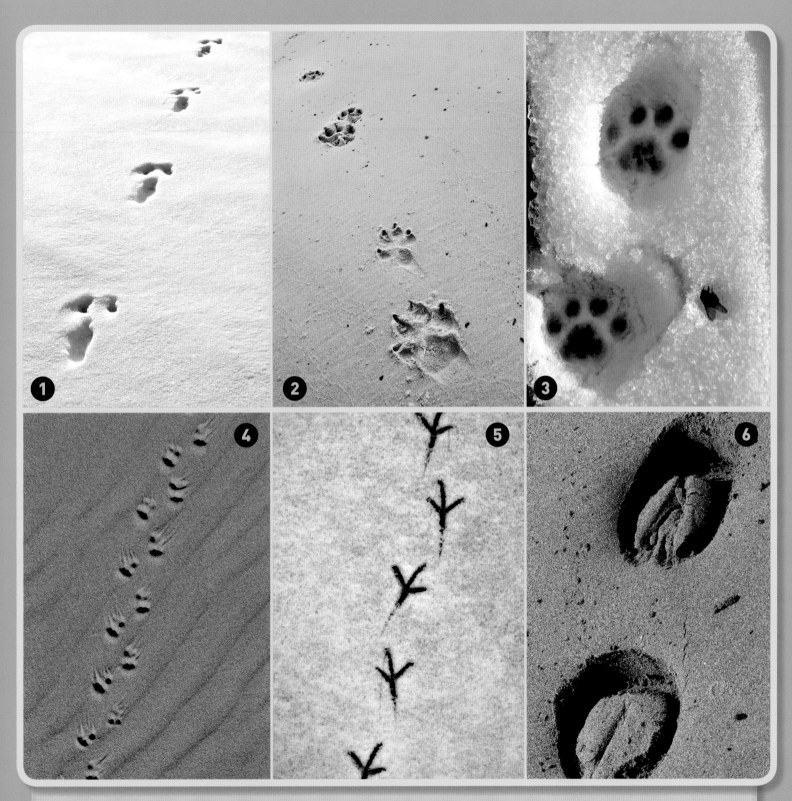

MAKING TRACKS

Try your hand at being a pet detective. Match the pet tracks with the pet.

A bird
B cat
C dog
D chameleon
E rabbit
F horse

PHOTO FINISH

ONE OF THE MOST INTERESTING **DOGS I EVER MET WAS BETSY.** She is a beautiful border collie and the pet of a couple in Austria, named the Schaefers. They let Betsy join in experiments so humans can learn more about what goes on in our pets' minds.

The scientists discovered that Betsy knows the names of more than 300 toys; she learns a new word whenever the Schaefers give her a new toy. She never forgets the names of her old toys. If you ask Betsy to bring Lobster, a rubber toy, she will search through all of her toys to find that one.

I met Betsy in her home when I was writing a story for *National Geographic* magazine. Two scientists were also visiting Betsy to give her a new test. Mrs. Schaefer sat on the floor with Betsy in front of her. She held up a photograph of a new toy for Betsy to see: a small, brightly colored Frisbee. Mrs. Schaefer gave it the name Frisbee. "Look, Betsy," she said. "This is Frisbee." Betsy cocked her head and made a tiny whimper. She knew that Mrs. Schaefer was teaching her something new, but she wasn't sure what it was. Mrs. Schaefer pointed to the picture and repeated the name Frisbee several times. Betsy kept her ears pointing up, listening to her owner.

Then Mrs. Schaefer said, "Okay, Betsy. Go find Frisbee." Betsy trotted into the kitchen where the scientists had placed five toys and five photographs of toys. There was a photograph of Frisbee just like the one Mrs. Schaefer had shown Betsy, and there was a real Frisbee.

What do you think Betsy brought back to Mrs. Schaefer? If you guessed the real Frisbee, you're right! She came running back to her owner with the toy Frisbee in her mouth. Betsy knew that things, like toys, have names. And she knew the photograph wasn't the real toy!

AFTERWORD

WHEN MOTHER NATURE STRIKES,

PETS CAN SOMETIMES GO MISSING IN ACTION. Shelters that accommodate humans who've had to leave their homes can't always take care of pets too. Luckily, animal welfare organizations and volunteers stand ready to spring into action to save pets and try to reunite them with their owners. These tireless people set up mobile units, helicopter airlifts, boats, and temporary shelters for pets.

After Hurricane Katrina swept ashore in 2005, hundreds of thousands of animals had to be left behind when people abandoned their homes. The Humane Society of the United States, along with such groups as the Best Friends Animal Society and the Louisiana SPCA, arrived on the flooded scene to lend a hand. Approximately 8,000 animals were rescued from homes and streets, and hundreds were reunited with their owners. Prior to Katrina, there were no government requirements for evacuation teams to rescue pets. But after that disaster a new law was passed. The Pet Evacuation and Transportation Standards Act (PETS Act) now provides special consideration and funding for pet rescue.

Earthquakes are especially trying for pets and their people. In San Francisco, California, where quakes are common, a "no-pets-left-behind" policy ensures that when people are rescued, their dogs, rabbits, birds, and other animals will likely be rescued too. There's no such policy in Fukushima, Japan, and in 2011, when the government issued a mandatory evacuation of people

Volunteers in animal shelters help socialize cats, which includes petting them to get them ready for human contact. This cat was left homeless after Hurricane Katrina.

in a 12 to 18-mile (20 to 30-km) radius around a nuclear plant, an estimated 15,000 pets had to be left behind. Volunteers and pet owners were so determined to rescue those animals that they broke the law and entered the dangerous no-entry area to bring out as many stranded pets as they could.

Even social media like Facebook and Twitter can help. Some states, including Alabama and Texas, have posted photos of pets—both lost and found—following tornadoes and wildfires. Local animal shelters can upload photos of displaced pets as well. In any natural disaster, technology is helping to keep owners and their beloved pets together.

HOW TO
PREPARE YOUR PETS

PETS OFTEN HIDE DURING BAD WEATHER, so know their hiding places so you can find them quickly. Any pet that wears a collar needs a visible tag with up-to-date information. Microchipping is a permanent way to identify your pet, and it might increase the chances that you will be reunited after an emergency. Consider preparing a portable disaster kit for your pet that contains food in a waterproof container, water, medications, veterinary records, a carrier or leash, and some toys to reduce stress. Keep the kit in an accessible place so you will have what you need if you have to leave quickly with your pet. You can also put a Pet Alert sticker on a front window to alert responders that a pet might be inside.

A rescued dog in New Orleans says "thanks."

Aquariums are not only friendly homes for these tetra and discus fish, but they are beautiful to look at, too!

AN INTERACTIVE GLOSSARY

This house cat would rather roll over and purr than do homework.

THESE WORDS ARE
COMMONLY USED WHEN PEOPLE TALK

about pets. Use the glossary to learn what each word means and visit its page numbers to see the word used in context.

Ancestors
[PAGE 26]
Wild animals that lived long ago but are directly related to the pet

A dog's ancestor is which animal?
a. a cat
b. a wolf
c. a snake
d. a Chihuahua

Aquarium
[PAGES 7, 17, 38, 59]
A special habitat for fish and other animals that live in either salt water or fresh water

A saltwater aquarium would have fish from which body of water?
a. a stream
b. an ocean
c. a freshwater lake
d. a swimming pool

Body Language
[PAGE 36]
The way humans and animals communicate feelings through movements, gestures, and facial expressions instead of words

Common body language for showing you are angry is ____.
a. frowning
b. yawning
c. yelling
d. smiling

Breed
[PAGES 10, 13-14, 19, 39, 46-49]
A group of animals that have the same traits

Dogs of the same breed share which traits?
a. size
b. natural behavior
c. hair length
d. all of these

Companion
[PAGES 7, 9, 13, 22, 29]
A person or animal that keeps people company or is part of a group or family

Which companion was a favorite of sailors?
a. cats
b. parrots
c. fish
d. mermaids

Domesticated
[PAGE 10]
Tamed from the wild or raised to live with and help humans

Which of these is a domesticated animal?
a. an elephant
b. a shark
c. a cat
d. a cockroach

Feline
[PAGES 26-27]
A word that refers to cats or animals in the cat family

Which of these animals would be a feline pet?
a. a parakeet
b. a gerbil
c. a catfish
d. a kitten

Life span
[PAGE 43]
The average length of life for an animal or plant

Which group of animals typically lives only until its teens?
a. fish
b. snakes
c. cats
d. parrots

Mimic
[PAGES 17, 36, 38, 52]
To imitate or sound like something else

A parrot mimicking a person would be doing which of these?
a. saying words and phrases
b. applying for a job
c. walking the dog
d. cooking dinner

Reptiles
[PAGES 9, 11, 17, 39, 43]
Animals that breathe air, have scales, and lay eggs

Which of these is an example of a reptile?
a. An African Grey parrot
b. a corn snake
c. a Russian Dwarf hamster
d. a goldfish

Rodent
[PAGES 5, 13-15, 18, 39]
A type of mammal known for chewing—mice, hamsters, guinea pigs, and beavers are all rodents

Which rodent has the worst eyesight?
a. gerbils
b. chinchillas
c. mice
d. hamsters

Sanctuary
[PAGE 40]
A special type of animal habitat where certain wild, exotic, or special animals live and are kept away from people

Which of these animals would belong in a sanctuary?
a. a kitten
b. a rabbit
c. a tiger
d. a dog

Service Animal
[PAGE 35]
Animals specially trained to help people with disabilities

A service animal probably performs which of these tasks?
a. turning on the lights in a room
b. fetching a ball
c. burying a bone
d. driving a car

Shelter
[PAGES 29, 39, 41, 56]
A place where lost and abandoned animals go to either wait for their owner or find a new home

Which of these is an animal you will most likely find in a shelter?
a. a tropical fish
b. a parrot
c. a gerbil
d. a puppy

Veterinarian
[PAGE 38]
A doctor trained to care for animals

Which of these would be a good reason to see a veterinarian?
a. your dog eats your turkey sandwich
b. your snake sheds its skin
c. your parrot keeps saying "Hello"
d. your guinea pig starts coughing

ANSWERS: Ancestors: b; Aquarium: b; Body Language: a; Breed: d; Companion: a; Domesticated: a; Feline: c; Life span: c; Mimic: a; Reptiles: b; Rodent: d; Sanctuary: c; Service Animal: c; Shelter: a; Veterinarian: d

FIND OUT MORE

Find out more about which pet might be right for you with these websites.

ON THE WEB

ASPCA (American Society for the Prevention of Cruelty to Animals)

For nearly a century and a half, the ASPCA has been helping animals in almost every way imaginable.

www.aspca.org/Home/About-Us/programs-services

The Humane Society of the United States (HSUS)

If you visit the website of HSUS, you can find out more about domesticated, exotic, farm, and wild animals, and the work this organization does to be a voice for animals.

www.humanesociety.org

Kids Against Animal Cruelty (KAAC)

KAAC declares "We are Animal Rights Knights fighting for the rights of all animals!" It has chapters all over the U.S.

www.kidsagainstanimalcruelty.org

"Explorer" Virginia Morell

Virginia is on Facebook and has written many articles and some books, including her personal exploration to find the answer to this question: "What and how do animals think?"

www.facebook.com/virginia.morell.5

www.amazon.com/Virginia-Morell/e/B001HCZ348

American Kennel Club (AKC)

The AKC has a web newsletter with stories about responsible dog ownership, safety, and activities for kids and their dogs.

www.akc.org/public_education/kids_corner/kidscorner.cfm

The Petfinder Foundation

This organization has a dedicated YouTube channel with numerous videos, including ones about helping out at your local animal shelter.

www.youtube.com/petfinderfoundation

For " Suitcase," my first pet cat. – J.S.

Published by the National Geographic Society
John M. Fahey, *Chairman of the Board and*
  Chief Executive Officer
Declan Moore, *Executive Vice President; President,*
  Publishing and Travel
Melina Gerosa Bellows, *Executive Vice President;*
  Chief Creative Officer, Books, Kids, and Family

Prepared by the Book Division
Hector Sierra, *Senior Vice President and General Manager*
Nancy Laties Feresten, *Senior Vice President,*
  Kids Publishing and Media
Jay Sumner, *Director of Photography, Children's Publishing*
Jennifer Emmett, *Vice President, Editorial Director,*
  Children's Books
Eva Absher-Schantz, *Design Director,*
  Kids Publishing and Media
R. Gary Colbert, *Production Director*
Jennifer A. Thornton, *Director of Managing Editorial*

Staff for This Book
Kate Olesin, Robin Terry, *Project Editors*
Lynn Addison, *Project Manager*
James Hiscott, Jr., *Art Director*
Lori Epstein, Annette Kiesow, *Illustrations Editors*
Chad Tomlinson, *Designer*
Ariane Szu-Tu, *Editorial Assistant*
Callie Broaddus, *Design Production Assistant*
Hillary Moloney, *Associate Photo Editor*
Bianca Bowman, *Contributing Writer*
Nancie Majkowski, *Researcher*
Grace Hill, *Associate Managing Editor*
Joan Gossett, *Production Editor*
Lewis R. Bassford, *Production Manager*
Susan Borke, *Legal and Business Affairs*

Production Services
Phillip L. Schlosser, *Senior Vice President*
Chris Brown, *Vice President, NG Book Manufacturing*
George Bounelis, *Vice President, Production Services*
Nicole Elliott, *Manager*
Rachel Faulise, *Manager*
Robert L. Barr, *Manager*

The National Geographic Society is one of the world's largest nonprofit scientific and educational organizations. Founded in 1888 to "increase and diffuse geographic knowledge," the Society's mission is to inspire people to care about the planet. It reaches more than 400 million people worldwide each month through its official journal, *National Geographic*, and other magazines; National Geographic Channel; television documentaries; music; radio; films; books; DVDs; maps; exhibitions; live events; school publishing programs; interactive media; and merchandise. National Geographic has funded more than 10,000 scientific research, conservation, and exploration projects and supports an education program promoting geographic literacy.

For more information, please visit
www.nationalgeographic.com,
call 1-800-NGS LINE (647-5463),
or write to the following address:

National Geographic Society
1145 17th Street, N.W.
Washington, D.C. 20036-4688 U.S.A.

Visit us online at nationalgeographic.com/books

For librarians and teachers: ngchildrensbooks.org

More for kids from National Geographic:
kids.nationalgeographic.com

For information about special discounts for bulk
purchases, please contact National Geographic Books
Special Sales: ngspecsales@ngs.org

For rights or permissions inquiries, please contact
National Geographic Books Subsidiary Rights:
ngbookrights@ngs.org

Paperback ISBN: 978-1-4263-1362-2
Reinforced Library Binding ISBN: 978-1-4263-1363-9

Printed in Hong Kong
13/THK/1